Carol Doak's Starry Block of the Month

12 PAPER-PIECED QUILT BLOCKS ★ 3 PROJECTS

CAROL DOAK

Text copyright © 2025 by Carol Doak

Photography and artwork copyright © 2025 by C&T Publishing, Inc.

Publisher: Amy Barrett-Daffin

Creative Director: Gailen Runge

Senior Editor: Roxane Cerda

Editor: Gailen Runge

Cover/Book Designer: April Mostek

Production Coordinator: Tim Manibusan

Illustrator: Kirstie L. Pettersen

Photography Coordinator: Rachel Ackley

Photography by C&T Publishing, Inc., unless otherwise noted

Published by C&T Publishing, Inc., P.O. Box 1456, Lafayette, CA 94549

All rights reserved. No part of this work covered by the copyright hereon may be used in any form or reproduced by any means—graphic, electronic, or mechanical, including photocopying, recording, taping, or information storage and retrieval systems—without written permission from the publisher. The copyrights on individual artworks are retained by the artists as noted in *Carol Doak's Starry Block of the Month*. These designs may be used to make items for personal use only and may not be used for the purpose of personal profit. Items created to benefit nonprofit groups, or that will be publicly displayed, must be conspicuously labeled with the following credit: "Designs copyright © 2025 by Carol Doak from the book *Carol Doak's Starry Block of the Month* from C&T Publishing, Inc." Permission for all other purposes must be requested in writing from C&T Publishing, Inc.

Attention Copy Shops: Please note the following exception—publisher and author give permission to photocopy pages 17, 19, 21, 23, 25, 27, 29, 31, 33, 35, 37, and 39 for personal use only.

Attention Teachers: C&T Publishing, Inc., encourages the use of our books as texts for teaching. You can find lesson plans for many of our titles at ctpub.com or contact us at ctinfo@ctpub.com.

We take great care to ensure that the information included in our products is accurate and presented in good faith, but no warranty is provided, nor are results guaranteed. Having no control over the choices of materials or procedures used, neither the author nor C&T Publishing, Inc., shall have any liability to any person or entity with respect to any loss or damage caused directly or indirectly by the information contained in this book. For your convenience, we post an up-to-date listing of corrections on our website (ctpub.com). If a correction is not already noted, please contact our customer service department at ctinfo@ctpub.com or P.O. Box 1456, Lafayette, CA 94549.

Trademark (™) and registered trademark (®) names are used throughout this book. Rather than use the symbols with every occurrence of a trademark or registered trademark name, we are using the names only in the editorial fashion and to the benefit of the owner, with no intention of infringement.

Printed in the USA

10 9 8 7 6 5 4 3 2 1

Contents

Introduction   4

Gathering Tools and Supplies   5

Using Paper Foundations and Block-Front Drawings   6

Paper-Piecing Techniques   6
Measuring Fabric-Piece Size   7
Cutting Fabric Pieces   8
Step-by-Step Paper Piecing   9
Fixing Mistakes   11

Completing the Block   12
Joining Sections A and B   12
Joining the Sections   13
Removing the Paper   14

The Blocks   15
Gallery of Stars   15
January   16
February   18
March   20
April   22
May   24
June   26
July   28
August   30
September   32
October   34
November   36
December   38

Projects   40
Quilt Layout A   41
Quilt Layout B   42
Table Runner   43

About the Author   44

JANUARY 16

FEBRUARY 18

MARCH 20

APRIL 22

MAY 24

JUNE 26

JULY 28

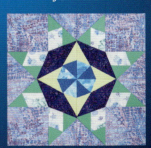

AUGUST 30

SEPTEMBER 32

OCTOBER 34

NOVEMBER 36

DECEMBER 38

Introduction

After I had written my most recent book, *60 Fabulous Paper-Pieced Stars*, featuring 12″ blocks created from eight paper-pieced sections, I had the desire to design even more star blocks. The designs may look intricate, but paper piecing makes it possible to sew these designs with absolute precision. After you've made just one star block, I think you will see how great this technique really is.

I designed 12 more blocks, each representing a month of the year, to share the fun of making paper-pieced stars that are easy to make yet create dramatic results. To share these fun designs, I started a Facebook Group, Carol Doak Bonus Block of the Month, offering up a block each month. In just a few short months, we had thousands of members worldwide making their version of each monthly block. The design variations based on fabric placement were just mind-blowing. Some members were beginners and some were advanced, but all enjoyed making these blocks. Some members shared that their guilds were selecting a block from the *60 Fabulous Paper-Pieced Stars* book to make a block each month and discovering the same variety. I could see the potential for other groups, guilds, and shops to enjoy this experience with the blocks I created for this online group, hence the *Carol Doak's Starry Block of the Month* was born.

Although the blocks represent the calendar months, you can begin the block of the month at the start of any month.

If you are a member of a guild, suggest this as a program for the year. Members can share their monthly blocks. It will be a great lesson in color placement and variation for the same design.

If you are a shop owner, this is a super monthly program for your customers to share their monthly blocks at the shop. You could end with a challenge to display the quilt tops made from the monthly blocks in the shop the following year.

If you just want a project to do with your friends, suggest this block of the month to share your blocks each month and have 12 blocks at the end of a year.

In Gathering Tools and Supplies (page 5) you will learn what items you need to make the blocks. In Using Paper Foundations and Block-Front Drawings (page 6), you'll learn that you can use a copy machine or scanner to reproduce the foundations.

In The Blocks (page 15), you will see a detailed cutting list for making one of each of the 12″ star blocks, plus color photos to inspire you.

At the end of the book, you'll find three project suggestions. One is a very straight-forward sampler. Even with a straight setting, the blocks can make the quilt shine! You'll also find another 12-block quilt that plays around with a fun-shaped internal border. Finally, I've included a 3-block table runner that gives you a perfect project for your practice blocks.

Gathering Tools and *Supplies*

Having the right tools to do the job can mean the difference between fun and frustration. The following items will make paper piecing the star blocks fun.

6″ Add-A-Quarter Ruler: This tool is invaluable for pre-trimming the fabric pieces.

Utility knife: (such as an X-Acto knife) Use this tool to undo seams easily.

Open-toe presser foot: This foot provides good visibility so you can see the line as you are stitching. If you don't have one, don't worry, you can still paper piece. It's just a "nice to have" item.

Carol Doak's Foundation Paper (C&T Publishing): Use this lightweight paper when you copy the foundation piecing designs. It holds up during the sewing process and removes easily. (See page 44.)

Postcard or card stock: Use a sturdy postcard or card stock to fold the paper back on the foundation before trimming the fabric pieces. The card that comes with the Carol Doak Foundation Paper is perfect for this purpose.

Rotary cutter and rotary mat: The large rotary cutter (45mm) is the most effective with these star patterns, because you will often be cutting through four layers of fabric and paper.

Rotary rulers: The 6″ × 12″ and the 6″ × 6″ rotary rulers are helpful for cutting the fabric and trimming the sections.

Scotch brand removable tape: This tape will be your new best friend if you need to repair your paper foundation.

Sewing thread: Use a standard 50-weight sewing thread. Match the thread color to the value of the fabrics. White, medium gray, and black can be used for most blocks. If both dark and light values are used equally within a block, choose the darker thread.

Flat-headed pins: Use these to hold the fabric pieces in place. The flat head will not get in your way when trimming.

Size 90/14 sewing machine needles: The larger needle will help to perforate the paper so it is easy to remove later.

Small light: This will be helpful when you want to center a fabric element in the #1 position and to see through the foundation.

Small stick-on notes: Label your stacks of cut fabric pieces with these. They will keep you organized and save you time.

Curved pointed snips: These are great for removing the top and bottom threads simultaneously. From the paper side, pull up the thread to bring up the bottom thread and snip.

Tweezers: These will come in handy to remove tiny bits of paper.

Using Paper Foundations and *Block-Front Drawings*

Each star block requires four copies each of the section A and B triangles. One way to make paper foundations is to photocopy the designs on a copy machine. Be sure to make all the copies for your project with the same copy machine from the original designs. For a nominal fee, most copy shops will remove the binding of this book and three-hole-punch the pages or spiral bind it to make using it on a copy machine even easier. If you have a scanner, you can also scan the foundation page into your device and print your foundations. Always test the accuracy of the copy or scan before using it.

A copy machine will also permit you to enlarge or reduce the size of the foundation. A digital image created by a scanner will also permit you to print the foundation larger or smaller if you wish.

The paper you use for foundation piecing should hold up while sewing and be easy to remove. If in doubt, test your paper by sewing through it with a size 90/14 needle and a stitch length of 18 to 20 stitches per inch. If it tears as you sew, it is too weak. If it doesn't tear easily when pulled after sewing, it is too strong. The paper does not need to be translucent. The light from your sewing machine is sufficient to see through the blank side of the paper to the lines on the other side. *Carol Doak's Foundation Paper* (by C&T Publishing) works beautifully for these star blocks.

After you make 4 copies of sections A and B, cut the triangles ½″ from the outside solid line. To do this quickly and easily, pin the center of the sections together using a flat-headed pin. Use your rotary ruler and cutter to trim. You do not dull your blade doing this if you use *Carol Doak's Foundation Paper*. Remove the pin.

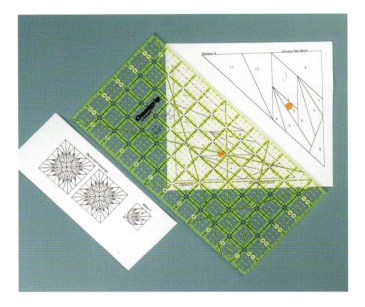

The small block-front drawings at the bottom of the pattern pages show how the star blocks will appear when they are completed. Use these blocks to experiment with color and design choices. One set of decisions can result in a very different star block from another set of decisions. I think you will be amazed at the variations available with these designs just by using different color and value placement. The block-front drawings are the reverse images of the foundations.

Paper-Piecing Techniques

Measuring Fabric-Piece Size

The good news is that there is a cutting list for making one of each 12″ star block. The measurements are generous to allow room for easy placement and any shifting that might occur while you sew. You always have the option to cut pieces larger.

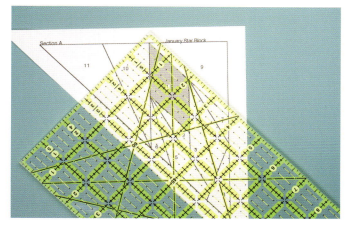

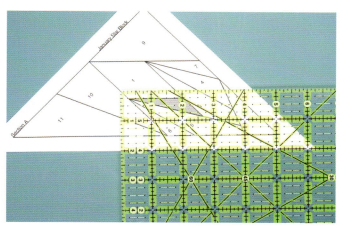

However, if you decide to enlarge or reduce the designs, you will want to know how to measure the fabric pieces. To measure the first piece, place a rotary ruler over the area marked #1 in the same way you will place the #1 fabric. You can see how big the fabric piece needs to be, including a generous seam allowance. I allow at least ¾″ total for seam allowances. Write the measurement on your foundation.

To measure the subsequent fabric pieces, place the ¼″ line on the rotary ruler on the seam you will sew and let the ruler fall over the area of the next piece. Add ½″ on the opposing sides. Look through the ruler to see how big the piece needs to be, including a generous seam allowance on all sides. Write the measurement on your foundation.

For half-square triangles, measure the short side of the triangle and add 1¼″ to that measurement. Cut a square the size of the short side of the triangle plus 1¼″ and cut it once diagonally.

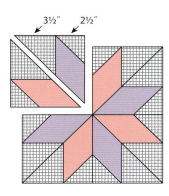

When the short side measures 3½″, add 1¼″ for seam allowances to cut a square 4¾″ × 4¾″. Cut in half diagonally to make two half-square triangles.

When the short side measures 2½″, add 1¼″ for seam allowances to cut a square 3¾″ × 3¾″. Cut in half diagonally to make two half-square triangles.

Cutting Fabric Pieces

Once your fabric is selected, it is time to rotary cut your fabric pieces. Remember, each star block has a cutting list. If you prefer different colors from the ones listed, simply substitute your fabric choices for the ones in the chart. And if you want to cut your pieces larger to give yourself more wiggle room with placement, that is fine, too.

To cut several pieces at one time, fold the fabric twice and cut a strip across the width. If you need only a few pieces, cut a shorter strip.

As the pieces are cut, label them with stick-on notes to indicate the location number and section. Since the fabric is folded, the pieces will be right side up and wrong side up. Take the time to arrange them so they are all right side up. This saves time when sewing.

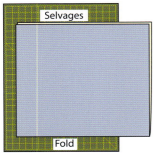

Fabric folded once

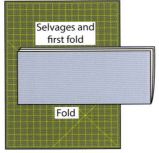

Fabric folded twice to cut strips

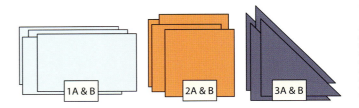

Many of the star blocks require half-square triangles for the background triangles. These are easily cut from 4¾″ and 3¾″ squares. Fold the fabric twice and cut a 4¾″-wide strip across the width. Turn the strip and remove the fold and selvage edges. Cut four squares 4¾″ × 4¾″. Remember, since you're cutting four layers of fabric at a time, you will be cutting four squares at once. Cut the squares once diagonally to make eight triangles. Cut four squares, 3¾″ × 3¾″, from the remainder of the strip, and cut once diagonally to make eight triangles.

After the fabric pieces are cut and labeled, place them on a tray in numerical order. This allows you to move them from the cutting area to the sewing machine area easily. I find that the trays you often get fruit and meats on at the supermarket are perfect for this purpose. Be sure to wash them well.

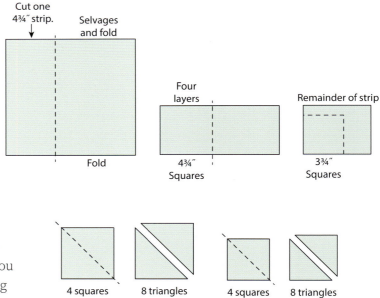

8 Carol Doak's Starry Block of the Month

Step-by-Step Paper Piecing

With your foundations copied and trimmed, your fabric selected, cut and labeled, you are now ready to begin paper piecing the sections for your star block. The numbered and lined side of the foundation is the reverse (or mirror image) of the finished block. This often confuses beginners to paper piecing because they look at the lined side and try to think in reverse. The key is to look through the blank side of the foundation to the lines on the other side. This way, what you see is what you get and you do not need to think in reverse.

In the following photographs, translucent tracing paper is used as the foundation for the January Star block, Section A, so you can see the lines through the blank side of the paper.

1. Use a size 90/14 sewing machine needle, an open-toe presser foot for good visibility and a stitch length of 18 to 20 stitches to the inch. The larger needle and smaller stitch length will aid you in removing the paper easily.

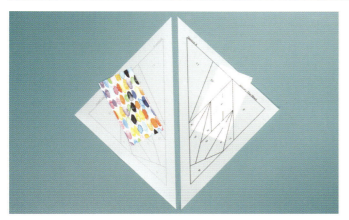

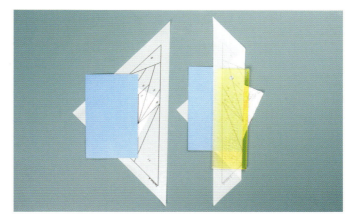

2. Using the light on your sewing machine (or an additional light source), look through the **blank side** of the paper to place fabric piece #1 **right side up** over the area marked #1. Looking through the lined side, make sure the fabric piece covers area #1 and extends at least ¼″ beyond all seam lines. Pin in place. I always pin parallel to the seam line I will sew.

3. Place the postcard on the line between #1 and #2 over the #1 area, and fold the paper back to expose the excess fabric beyond the seam line. Place an Add-A-Quarter ruler on the fold.

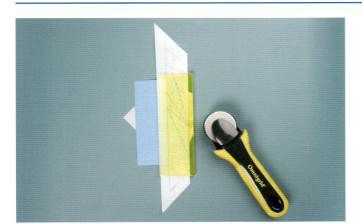

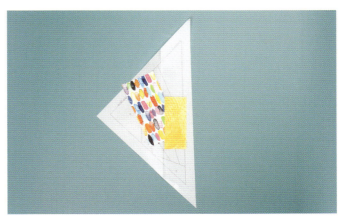

4. Trim the excess fabric ¼″ from the fold. The lip on this ruler prevents it from slipping as you trim. You can also align the ¼″ on a rotary ruler with the fold to trim.

5. Looking through the blank side of the paper to the design on the other side, place fabric #2 **right side up** over area #2. This step allows you to ballpark the placement of the #2 fabric.

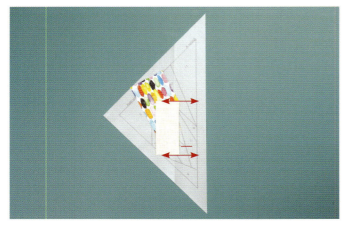

After piece #2 is properly positioned, flip it right sides together with the just-trimmed edge of piece #1. Looking through the blank side of the paper again, check that the end of #2 extends beyond the end of the seam line of #2 on the foundation. The red double arrows show where the fabric will go. The straight red line shows the bottom end of the #2 piece. Pin in place.

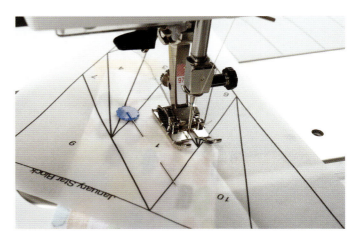

6. Place the foundation under the presser foot and sew on the seam line between #1 and #2. beginning about ½˝ before the seam and extending the stitching the same distance beyond the end of the seam line.

7. Remove the pins and open piece #2. Press with a dry iron on a cotton setting. If you are using heat-sensitive fabrics, use a pressing cloth or lower the temperature of the iron. Cover your ironing surface with a piece of scrap fabric to protect it from any ink that may transfer from photocopies. If you are getting a lot of ink transfer, reduce the iron temperature. *Caution:* Never press the printed side of the foundation as the iron will smear the ink.

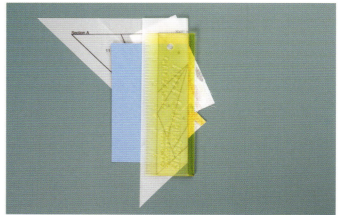

8. Place the postcard on the next line you will sew. This is where line #3 adjoins the previous pieces. Fold the paper back exposing the excess fabric. If necessary, pull the extending stitches away from the paper foundation to fold the paper. Place the Add-a-Quarter ruler on the fold and trim ¼˝ from the fold.

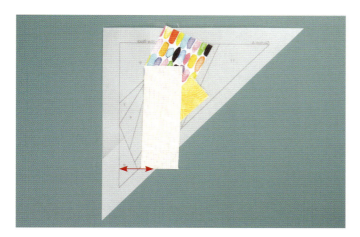

9. Place fabric #3 **right side up** over area #3 to check for proper placement. Place the fabric right sides together with the just-trimmed edges of pieces #1 and #2. See how the fabric extends to cover the end of #3 plus seam allowance? Sew on the line and press open.

10. Continue with the subsequent pieces by placing the card on the next line you will sew, trim using the Add-A-Quarter, position the next fabric **right side up** over the piece it will cover to ballpark placement, flip right sides together along the edge you just trimmed, and sew on the line. A good reminder of the sequence is Trim, Sew, Press. Place triangle #9 **right side up** over area #9 to check for placement, and then flip it right sides together along the just-trimmed edge. Align the corner of the fabric triangle with the corner of the triangle printed on the foundation. Sew and press open. Complete the block by adding the final two pieces.

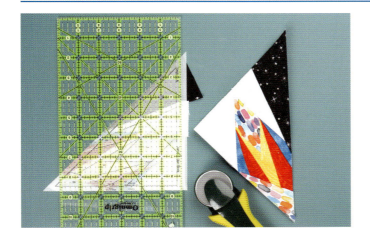

11. Trim the foundation ¼″ from the outside **solid** line as follows: Place the ¼″ line on your rotary ruler on the outside seam line. Trim the long side of the triangle first. Then trim the two short sides.

Fixing Mistakes

It's easy to fix a mistake should you need to remove a piece. Place a piece of Scotch Brand removable tape on the seam line where you will remove the piece. The tape will keep the paper intact. From the fabric side, lift the piece to be removed until the stitches at the end of the seam are visible. Lightly touch the stitches with the utility knife to cut them as you keep upward pressure on the fabric being removed. Once the piece is removed, you can resew the seam and the tape is your new foundation. Caution: Do not touch the tape with your iron.

Completing the *Block*

Joining Sections A and B

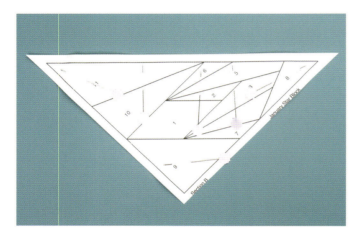 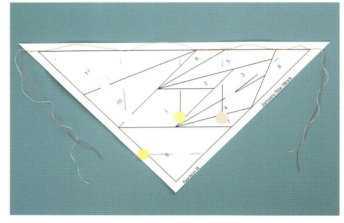

When the A and B sections are completed and trimmed, it is time to join them to make quarter blocks. I am going to depict this with printed foundations (not completed wedges), so you can focus on the joining of the seams. Place the A and B sections together, right sides facing. Place the long side down on a hard surface to align them. Hold the papers and pin the right-angle corner. Walk your fingers along the long sides to align them and pin at the beginning, at each matching point or every 3″, and the end point. Place pins away from the seam line.

Trust me, you'll definitely want to follow this basting step before you join the sections with the small stitch. Basting allows you to check that the seams match before you sew them and it prevents the sections from shifting.

To baste, increase the stitch length to about 8 stitches per inch. Baste about 1″ on the line at the beginning of the line, move to any matching points or every 3″ if there are no matching points along the seam and at the end.

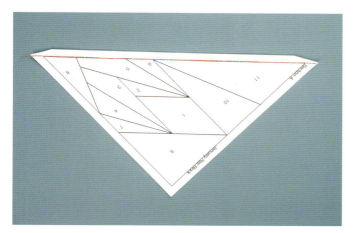
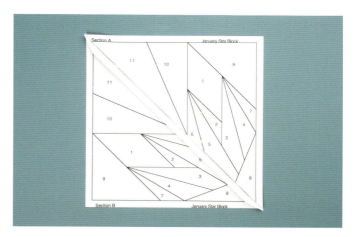

Remove the basted triangles from the sewing machine and check that you have basted on the seam line. Open up the sections and check for a good match. If they are good, sew with the small stitch. If one or more are not good, clip the basting thread for that matching point, adjust and baste again until the match is good and then sew with the small stitch.

Clip the seam allowances at an angle to reduce bulk where the centers and corners will come together.

Open and press the seam allowances toward section B from the fabric side. Join the four quarters for one star block in the same way, clipping the dog ears that extend beyond the foundation.

Joining the Sections

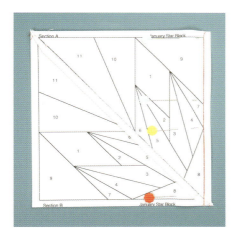
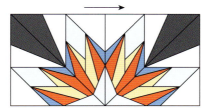
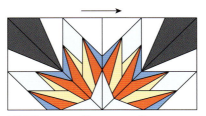
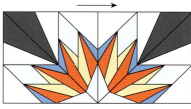
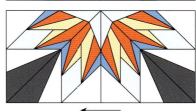

Place two quarters right sides together. Pin; baste at the beginning, at any matching points or every 3″ if there are no matching points, and at the end; check for a good match. When you are happy with the match, sew with a small stitch to make one half of the block. Join the remaining two quarters to make the other half block.

Middle seam allowances finger pressed to the right.

Looking at the fabric sides of the half blocks, finger press the middle seam allowance for both halves to the right.

Middle seam allowances go in opposing directions to lock in place.

When you rotate one half block to join them, the middle seam allowances will go in opposing directions.

Completing the Block

With right sides facing, pin the two halves together. Pin each end. Pin the matching points from the ends to the middle. Pin the middle last with seam allowances going in opposite directions. Baste at the beginning, at any matching points or every 3″ if there are no matching points, and at the end. Check you have a good match, and sew with a smaller stitch. I found that if I decreased the stitch length to twenty-five stitches per inch just at the center seam, it gave an even tighter match.

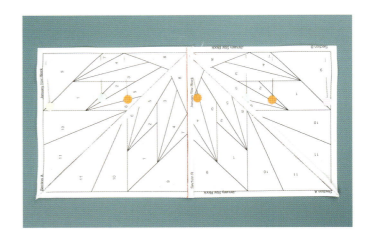

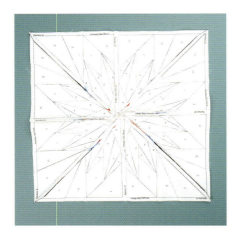
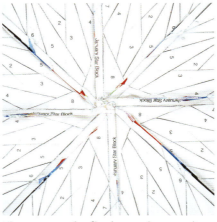

Finger press the final seam in opposite directions to follow the spiral of seam allowances on the back of the block.

From the paper side, finger press the final seam in opposite directions following the spiral of the seam allowances. Turn the block over and press.

Removing the Paper

Do not remove the paper until the block is joined to other blocks or other straight-grain fabric pieces. The outside seam lines act as a sewing guide and the paper stabilizes the blocks. To remove the paper, begin at the center portion of the block and gently tug diagonally to pull the paper away from the stitching lines. Use tweezers to remove any caught paper. You can ignore really tiny bits.

The Blocks

The Gallery of Stars (below) presents all 12 star blocks together. Following the Gallery of Stars are photographs and a cutting list for each of the star blocks. Digital reproductions show how four blocks will look when joined.

The blocks range from 64 pieces for August to 128 pieces for December. December is not more difficult to make, it only takes a little longer to complete.

The cutting list provided for each star block is for making one block. If you use different colors but the same fabric placements, follow the list substituting your color choice. If you use different fabric placements, simply create a new cutting list using the sizes provided for each number on the foundation.

The ◺ symbol in the cutting list indicates you should cut the squares once diagonally to create two half-square triangles (see page 7).

The foundation pages include a full-size paper piecing foundation for each block. They are the reverse image of the finished block. Each section is labeled A or B and the Month of the block. Make four copies of each A and B to make one block (see page 6).

On the bottom of each page are the block-front drawings to show how the completed A and B quarter sections will look and then two copies of the finished blocks. You can use these to experiment with color placements.

Gallery of Stars

January Star

88 pieces

The following fabric cutting list is for one 12″ star block.

Fabric	Pieces	Piece Dimensions	Piece Number	Block Section
Dark blue	8	2″ × 4″	1	A, B
	16	1″ × 3¼″	6, 7	A, B
Light teal	8	1¼″ × 4½″	5	A, B
Light green	8	1¼″ × 4″	4	A, B
Light peach	8	1¼″ × 3″	2	A, B
Medium peach	8	1½″ × 4¼″	3	A, B
Medium red	4	1½″ × 3½″	8	A
Light red	4	1½″ × 3½″	8	B
Green	8	2″ × 4½″	10	A, B
	4	3¾″ × 3¾″ ◺	9	A, B
Blue print	8	2½″ × 5¾″	11	A, B

◺ indicates to cut the squares to size and cut once diagonally.

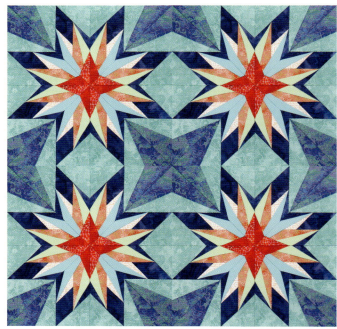

Section A January Star Block

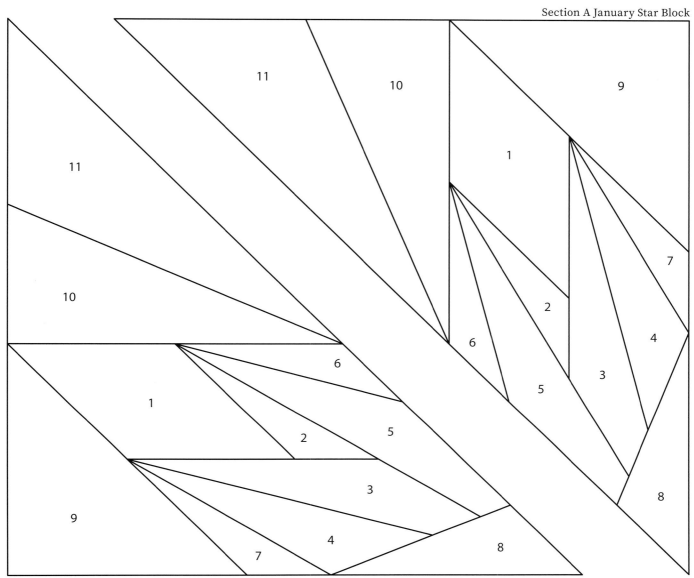

Section B January Star Block

Block-front drawings

Make 4.
Use this 1″ square to confirm your accurate copy size.

The Blocks 17

February Star

80 pieces

The following fabric cutting list is for one 12″ star block.

Fabric	Number of Pieces	Piece Dimensions	Piece Number	Block Section
Medium red	4	1½″ × 2½″	1	B
Dark red	4	1½″ × 2½″	1	A
White	16	1¼″ × 2″	2, 3	A, B
Medium blue	4	2¼″ × 3½″	5	B
Dark blue	4	2¼″ × 3½″	5	A
Black	8	1¼″ × 3″	7	A, B
Black	8	1¾″ × 4¼″	8	A, B
White/gray print	8	2¼″ × 3″	4	A, B
White/gray print	8	2¼″ × 3¾″	6	A, B
White/gray print	4	3¾″ × 3¾″ ◺	9	A, B
White/gray print	4	4¾″ × 4¾″ ◺	10	A, B

◺ indicates to cut the squares to size and cut once diagonally.

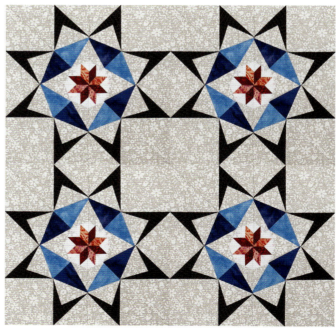

Section A February Star Block

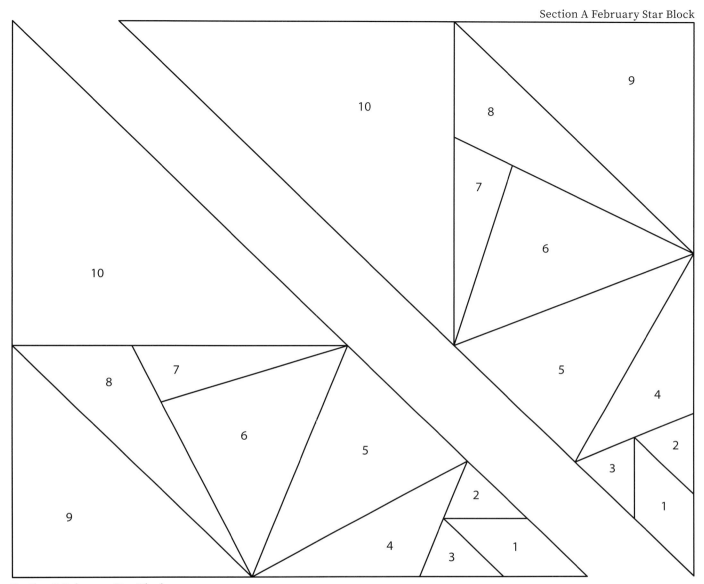

Section B February Star Block

Block-front drawings

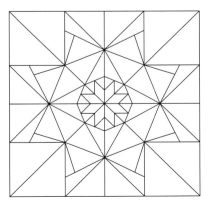

Make 4.
Use this 1″ square to confirm your accurate copy size.

The Blocks

March Star

112 Pieces

The following fabric cutting list is for one 12″ star block.

Fabric	Pieces	Piece Dimensions	Piece Number	Block Section
Assorted greens	16	1¼″ × 2½″	2, 4	A, B
	8	1¼″ × 3¾″	8	A, B
	8	1¼″ × 4½″	9	A, B
	8	2″ × 4½″	6	A, B
Peach	4	1¼″ × 3″	12	B
Dark red	4	1¼″ × 3″	12	A
Pale yellow	8	1½″ × 2½″	1	A, B
	8	1¼″ × 4″	7	A, B
	32	1″ × 2½″	3, 5, 10, 11	A, B
Green print	4	3¾″ × 3¾″ ◳	13	A, B
	4	4¾″ × 4¾″ ◳	14	A, B

◳ *indicates to cut the squares to size and cut once diagonally.*

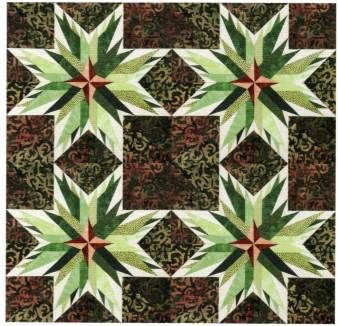

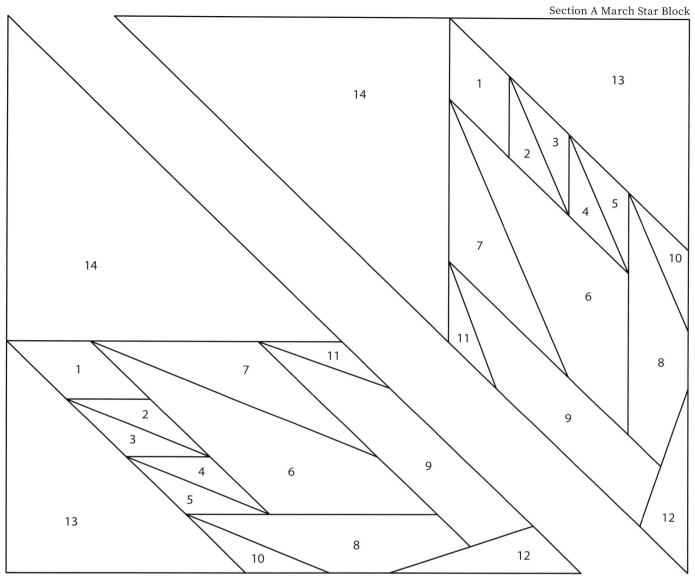

Section A March Star Block

Section B March Star Block

Block-front drawings

Make 4.
Use this 1″ square to confirm your accurate copy size.

The Blocks

April Star

96 Pieces

The following fabric cutting list is for one 12˝ star block.

Fabric	Number of Pieces	Piece Dimensions	Piece Number	Block Section
Green solid	8	1¼˝ × 3˝	9	A, B
Green print	8	1½˝ × 4½˝	10	A, B
Dark pink	8	1¼˝ × 3½˝	5	A, B
Light pink	8	1½˝ × 4˝	6	A, B
Yellow, green print	8	2¼˝ × 2¼˝	4	A, B
Gold	8	1¼˝ × 2¼˝	1	A, B
Blue	16	1½˝ × 1½˝	2, 3	A, B
	16	1½˝ × 3¾˝	7, 8	A, B
Black	2	3¾˝ × 3¾˝ ◺	11	A
	2	4¾˝ × 4¾˝ ◺	12	A
White	2	3¾˝ × 3¾˝ ◺	11	B
	2	4¾˝ × 4¾˝ ◺	12	B

◺ *indicates to cut the squares to size and cut once diagonally.*

22 Carol Doak's Starry Block of the Month

Section A April Star Block

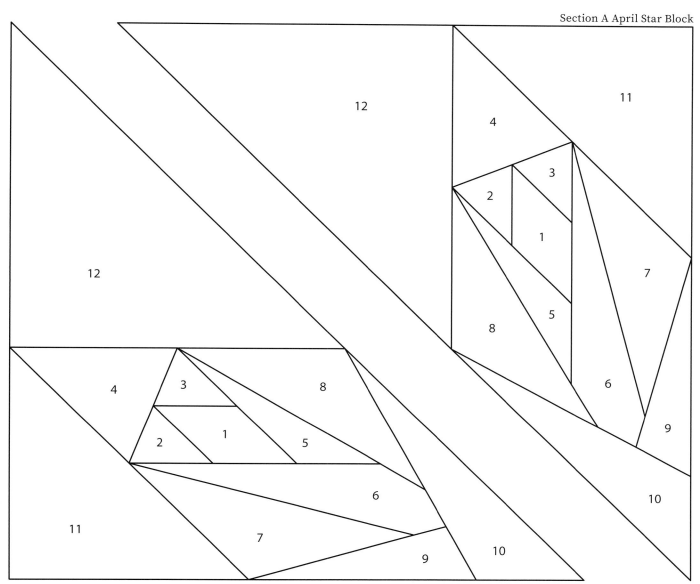

Section B April Star Block

Block-front drawings

Make 4.
Use this 1″ square to confirm your accurate copy size.

The Blocks 23

May Star

80 pieces

The following fabric cutting list is for one 12″ star block.

Fabric	Number of Pieces	Piece Dimensions	Piece Number	Block Section
Pink	8	1½″ × 2½″	4	A, B
Light blue	8	2″ × 2¾″	2	A, B
Medium blue	8	2″ × 4″	3	A, B
Black	8	1½″ × 2″	1	A, B
Black	16	1½″ × 3¾″	5, 6	A, B
White	8	1½″ × 3″	7	A, B
White	8	1¾″ × 4″	8	A, B
Print	4	3¾″ × 3¾″ ◨	9	A, B
Print	4	4¾″ × 4¾″ ◨	10	A, B

◨ *indicates to cut the squares to size and cut once diagonally.*

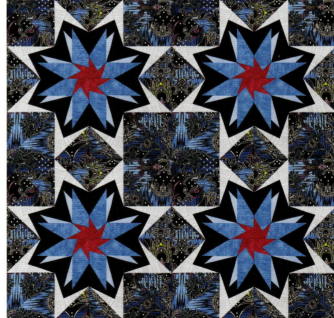

Section A May Star Block

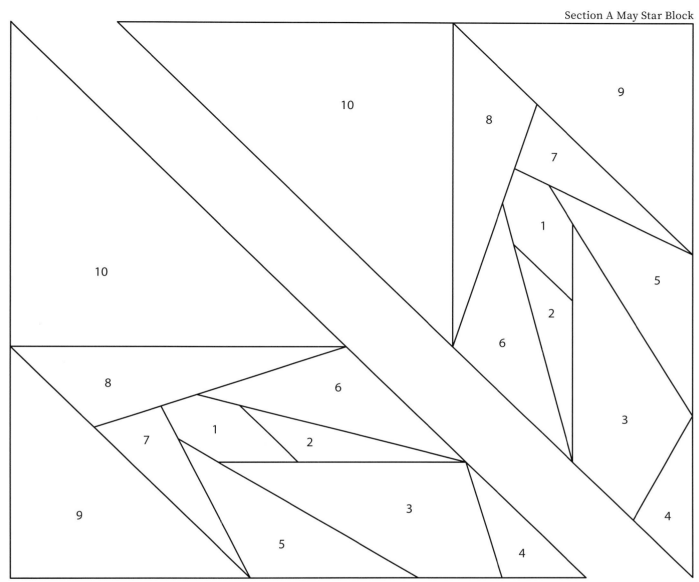

Section B May Star Block

Block-front drawings

Make 4.
Use this 1″ square to confirm your accurate copy size.

The Blocks **25**

June Star

72 pieces

The following fabric cutting list is for one 12″ star block.

Fabric	Number of Pieces	Piece Dimensions	Piece Number	Block Section
White print	16	1″ × 3½″	6, 7	A, B
	8	2″ × 4″	1	A, B
Light green	8	1½″ × 3½″	2	A, B
Purple	8	1¼″ × 2½″	3	A, B
Medium blue	8	1½″ × 5″	4	A, B
Teal	8	1¼″ × 4½″	5	A, B
Black	4	3¾″ × 3¾″ ◺	8	A, B
	4	4¾″ × 4¾″ ◺	9	A, B

◺ indicates to cut the squares to size and cut once diagonally.

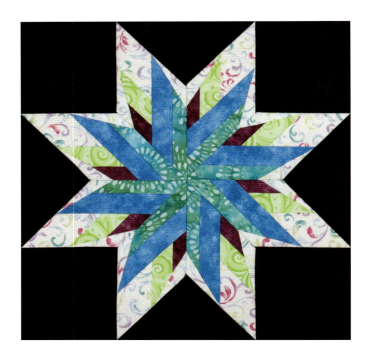
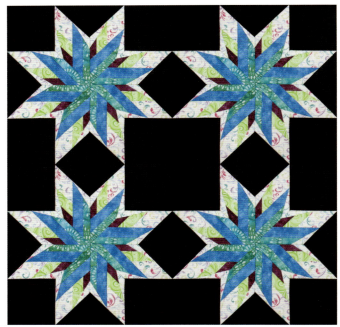

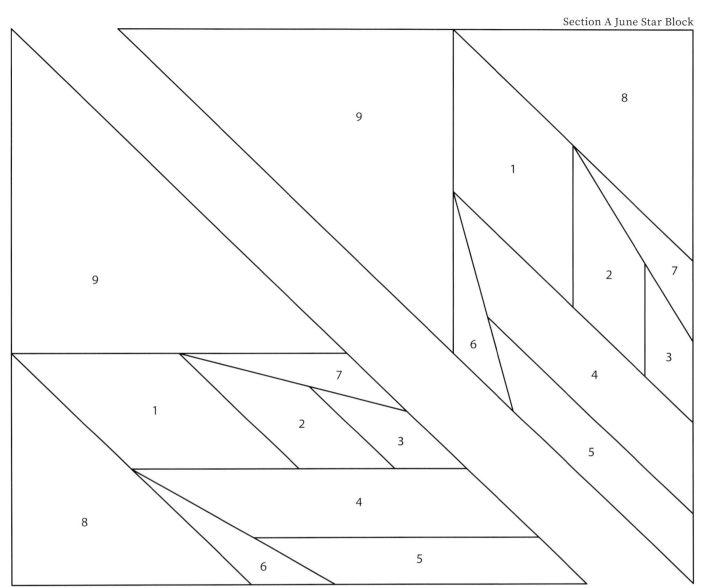

Section A June Star Block

Section B June Star Block

Block-front drawings

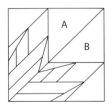

Make 4.
Use this 1˝ square to confirm your accurate copy size.

The Blocks

July Star

80 pieces

The following fabric cutting list is for one 12″ star block.

Fabric	Number of Pieces	Piece Dimensions	Piece Number	Block Section
Yellow	8	1¼″ × 2¼″	1	A, B
White	16	1½″ × 1½″	2, 3	A, B
Dark blue	8	2¼″ × 2¼″	8	A, B
Medium blue	4	2¼″ × 4″	7	A
Medium blue	4	1½″ × 2½″	6	B
Light blue	4	2¼″ × 4″	7	B
Light blue	4	1½″ × 2½″	6	A
Light peach	8	2″ × 3½″	5	A, B
Medium peach	8	2″ × 3″	4	A, B
Teal	4	3¾″ × 3¾″ ◨	9	A, B
Teal	4	4¾″ × 4¾″ ◨	10	A, B

◨ *indicates to cut the squares to size and cut once diagonally.*

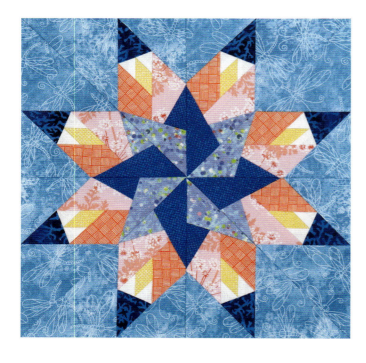
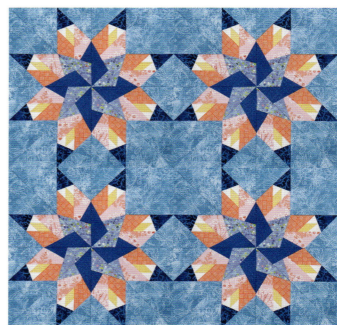

Section A July Star Block

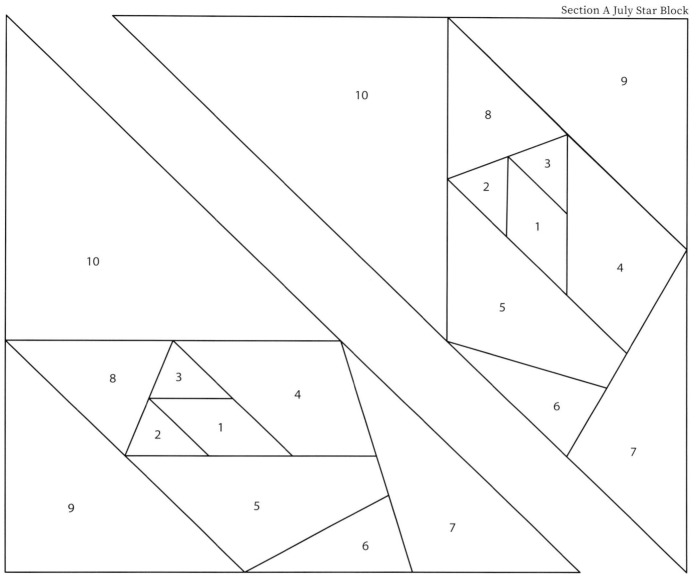

Section B July Star Block

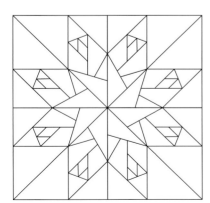

Block-front drawings

Make 4.
Use this 1″ square to confirm your accurate copy size.

The Blocks **29**

August Star

64 pieces

The following fabric cutting list is for one 12″ star block.

Fabric	Number of Pieces	Piece Dimensions	Piece Number	Block Section
Light blue	4	2¼″ × 2¼″	6	A
Medium blue	4	2¼″ × 2¼″	6	B
Yellow green	8	1½″ × 3¼″	5	A, B
Purple	8	2¼″ × 3½″	4	A, B
White	8	2″ × 3″	1	A, B
Green	8	2″ × 2½″	2	A, B
Green	8	2¼″ × 2¼″	3	A, B
Lavender print	4	3¾″ × 3¾″ ◻	7	A, B
Lavender print	4	4¾″ × 4¾″ ◻	8	A, B

◻ indicates to cut the squares to size and cut once diagonally.

Section A August Star Block

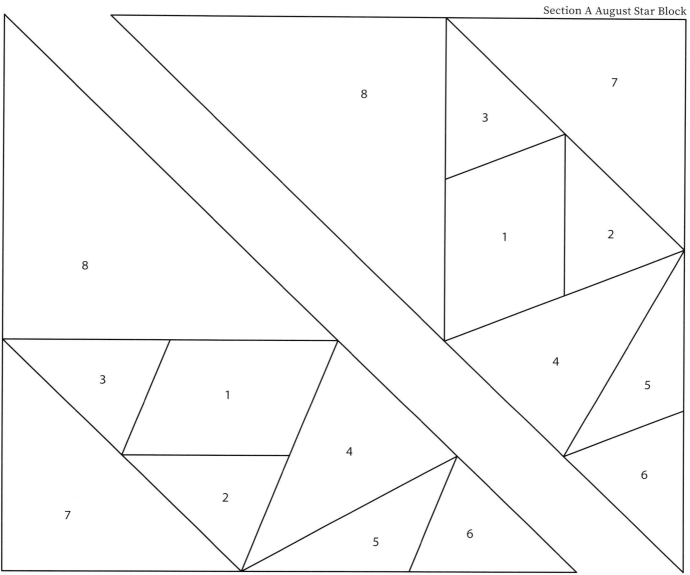

Section B August Star Block

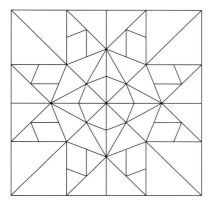

Block-front drawings

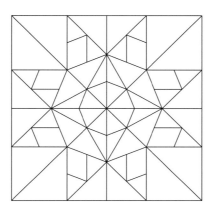

Make 4.
Use this 1″ square to confirm your accurate copy size.

The Blocks **31**

September Star

88 pieces

The following fabric cutting list is for one 12″ star block.

Fabric	Number of Pieces	Piece Dimensions	Piece Number	Block Section
Yellow	8	1½″ × 2½″	4	A, B
Orange	8	1½″ × 3½″	2	A, B
Orange print	8	1½″ × 3½″	3	A, B
Light green	8	1¼″ × 3″	8	A, B
Medium green	8	1½″ × 4¼″	9	A, B
Black	8	2¼″ × 2¼″	1	A, B
Black	8	2¼″ × 3¼″	7	A, B
Black	16	1¼″ × 2½″	5, 6	A, B
Red	4	3¾″ × 3¾″ ◺	10	A, B
Red	4	4¾″ × 4¾″ ◺	11	A, B

◺ indicates to cut the squares to size and cut once diagonally.

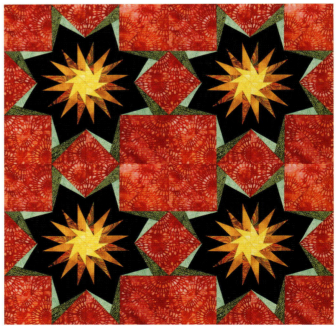

Section A September Star Block

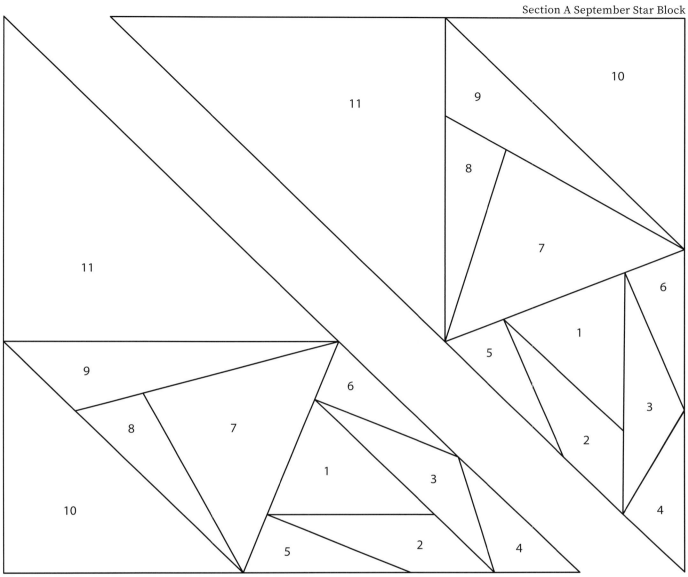

Section B September Star Block

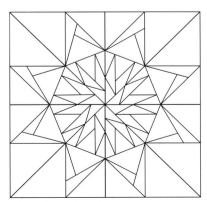

Block-front drawings

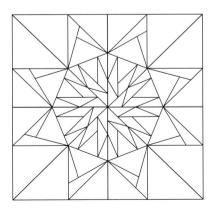

Make 4.
Use this 1″ square to confirm your accurate copy size.

The Blocks 33

October Star

68 pieces

The following fabric cutting list is for one 12″ star block.

Fabric	Number of Pieces	Piece Dimensions	Piece Number	Block Section
Blue	8	2″ × 4″	1	A, B
	8	1¾″ × 4½″	5	A, B
	8	1″ × 2¾″	4	A, B
Dark green	8	1¾″ × 4″	6	A
			7	B
Medium green	4	1½″ × 3″	6	B
Fuchsia	8	2″ × 4″	2	A, B
Pink	8	1½″ × 4″	3	A, B
Green/yellow print	4	3¾″ × 3¾″ ◨	7	A
			8	B
	4	4¾″ × 4¾″ ◨	8	A
			9	B

◨ indicates to cut the squares to size and cut once diagonally.

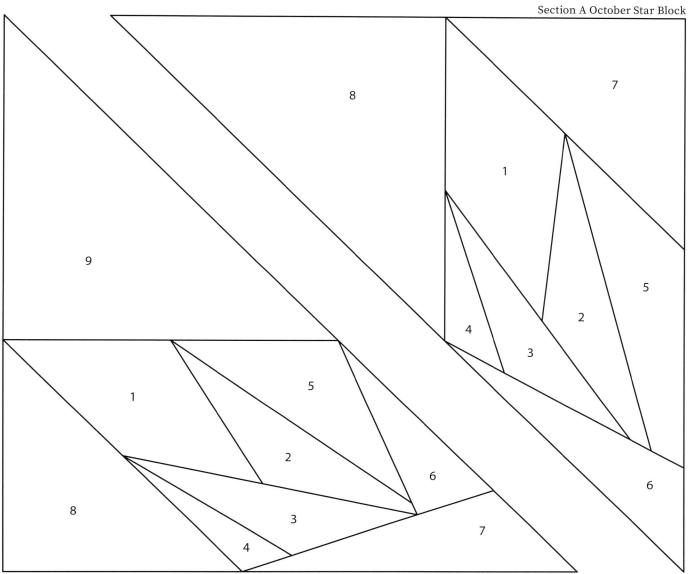

Section A October Star Block

Section B October Star Block

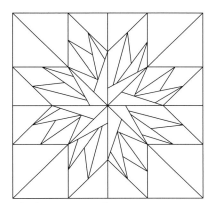

Block-Front Drawings

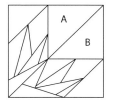

Make 4.
Use this 1″ square to confirm your accurate copy size.

The Blocks **35**

November Star

80 pieces

The following fabric cutting list is for one 12″ star block.

Fabric	Number of Pieces	Piece Dimensions	Piece Number	Block Section
Light green	8	1¼″ × 2½″	3	A, B
Medium green	8	1¼″ × 2½″	2	A, B
Teal	8	1¼″ × 3″	5	A, B
Medium red	8	1¼″ × 4″	6	A, B
Yellow	16	1¼″ × 4″	7, 8	A, B
Dark red	8	2″ × 4″	1	A, B
Dark red	8	2¼″ × 2¼″	4	A, B
Multi print	4	3¾″ × 3¾″ ◻	9	A, B
Multi print	4	4¾″ × 4¾″ ◻	10	A, B

◻ indicates to cut the squares to size and cut once diagonally.

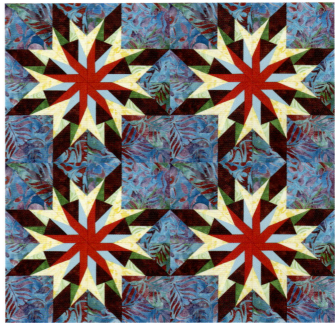

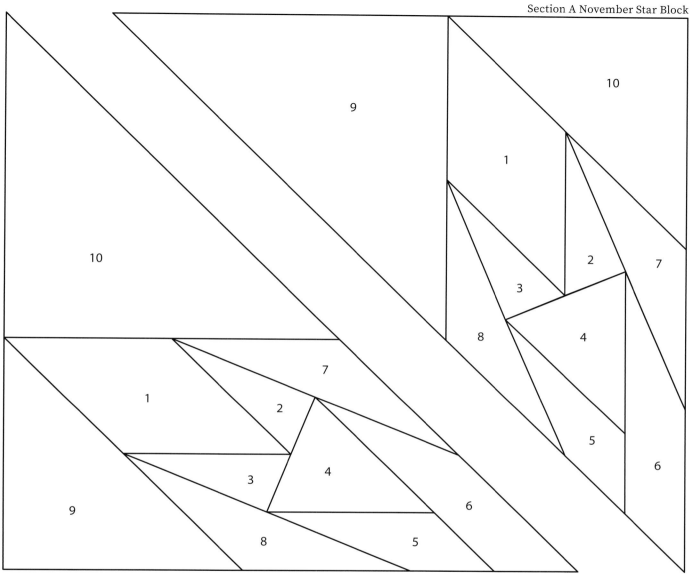

Section B November Star Block

Block-front drawings

Make 4.
Use this 1″ square to confirm
your accurate copy size.

The Blocks

December Star

128 pieces

The following fabric cutting list is for one 12″ star block.

Fabric	Pieces	Piece Dimensions	Piece Number	Block Section
White	8	1¼″ × 2¼″	1	A, B
	48	1″ × 2½″	4, 5, 8, 9, 12, 13	A, B
Dark green	16	1¼″ × 3¼″	10, 11	A, B
Medium green	8	1¼″ × 4″	7	A, B
Light green	8	1¼″ × 3″	6	A, B
Gold print	8	2¼″ × 2¼″	14	A, B
Blue	4	1¼″ × 3″	3	A
Purple print	4	1¼″ × 3″	3	B
Pink	8	1¼″ × 2¼″	2	A, B
Black	4	3¾″ × 3¾″ ◺	15	A, B
	4	4¾″ × 4¾″ ◺	16	A, B

◺ indicates to cut the squares to size and cut once diagonally.

Section A December Star Block

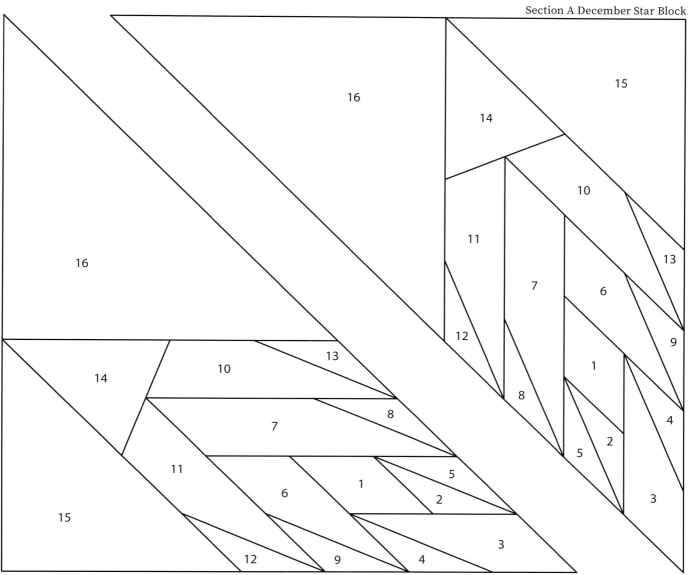

Section B December Star Block

Block-front drawings

Make 4.
Use this 1″ square to confirm your accurate copy size.

The Blocks **39**

Projects

QUILT LAYOUT A
Quilted by Kaylee Goyer

QUILT LAYOUT B

TABLE RUNNER

Quilt Layout A

Finished size: 55″ × 67″

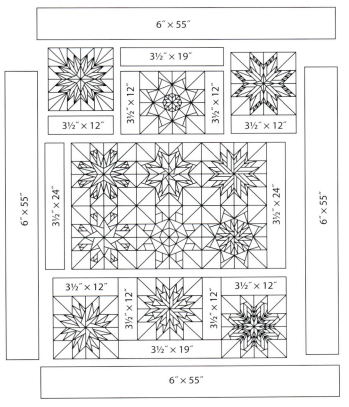

Finished sizes

YARDAGE REQUIREMENTS

Black outer border and binding: 1¾ yards

Blue inner border: ¾ yard

Backing fabric: 4 yards

Batting: 59″ × 71″

Cutting Chart

Fabric	Number to Cut	Size to Cut	Location
Blue	8	4″ × 12½″	Inner border
	2	4″ × 19½″	Inner top and bottom border
	2	4″ × 24½″	Inner side border
Black*	4	6½″ × 55½″	Outer border
	4	2¼″ × 63″	Binding
	1	2¼″ × 12″	Binding

*cut vertically

Quilt Layout B

Finished size: 48″ × 56″

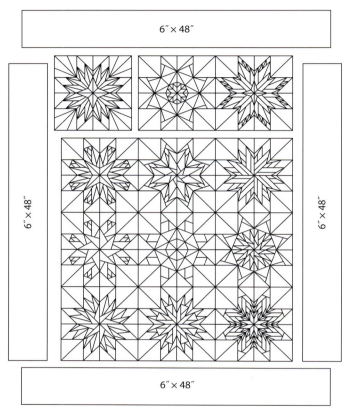

Finished sizes

YARDAGE REQUIREMENTS

Black outer border and binding: 1½ yards

Backing fabric: 3½ yards

Batting: 52″ × 60″

Cutting Chart

Fabric	Number to Cut	Size to Cut	Location
Black*	4	6½″ × 48″	Top, bottom, and side border
	4	2¼″ × 50″	Binding
	1	2¼″ × 25″	Binding

*cut vertically

Table Runner

Finished size: 17″ × 51″

The featured blocks in this table runner are February, April, and May; however, any months can be used. Once the top is pieced, you can sandwich it with batting and backing to quilt and then bind. You can also opt to just place the backing fabric right sides together with the patchwork top and stitch the perimeter, leaving a 6″ space open to turn the runner right side out and press. After pressing, stitch the open space closed.

YARDAGE REQUIREMENTS

Print setting triangles and binding: ¾ yard

Backing: 1½ yards

Batting: 21″ × 55″ (optional)

Cutting Chart

Fabric	Number to Cut	Size to Cut	Location
Print	1	18¼″ × 18¼″ (X)*	Side triangles
	2	9⅜″ × 9⅜″ (/)**	Corner triangles
	3	2¼″ × 40″	Binding

* (X) indicates to cut the square twice diagonally to create four quarter-square triangles

** (/) indicates to cut the squares once diagonally to create half-square triangles

About the Author

Carol Doak discovered her love of quilting in 1979 when she took a seven-week basic quilting class in Worthington, Ohio. She taught that class the following year and discovered that she also loved to teach others how to make quilts. Since then she has taught more than a million people to quilt through her best-selling books and DVDs and by traveling to teach around the world.

An innovator in the industry, Carol continues to wow the quilting world with her creative uses for paper piecing. Since writing her first paper-piecing book in 1993, she has designed more than 1,000 paper-pieced designs.

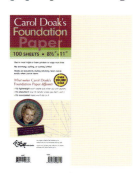

Her passion for designing and teaching is evident, whether you have taken a class from her or learned from her books and DVDs.

Carol's *Carol Doak's Foundation Paper* has sold more than 400,000 packages and has made paper piecing easier for countless quilters. The paper is available through C&T Publishing or ask for it at your local quilt shop.

Visit Carol online and follow on social media!
Website: caroldoak.com
Instagram: @carol.doak
Facebook: /CarolDoakQuilts

Other books and Products by Carol Doak

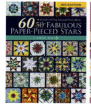    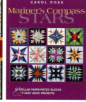   

If you enjoyed making these blocks, this book has more stars to enjoy and more techniques to learn.